QUEEN'S

An Architectural Legacy

Published 1995
The Institute of Irish Studies
The Queen's University of Belfast.

Grateful acknowledgement for financial assistance is made to Queen's 150

ISBN: 085389 594 5

© Authors

Research and layout by Paul Larmour
Watercolours and front cover by David Evans
Text by Paul Larmour and David Evans

Printed by W. & G. Baird Ltd., Antrim

Front cover: View of west front of the Lanyon Building, looking north.
Back cover: The 'Universal Knowledge' panel embodying the arms of the university, on the Sir William Whitla Hall.

British Library Cataloguing-in-Publication Data. A catalogue record for this book is available from the British Library.

QUEEN'S

An Architectural Legacy

David Evans and Paul Larmour

The Institute of Irish Studies
The Queen's University of Belfast
1995

The entrance tower of the Lanyon Building.

Preface

For most people the first and lasting image of Queen's is the long west façade of the Lanyon Building. It has all the virtues of the best Victorian architecture – bold massing, a memorable silhouette and plenty of interesting detail. It also strikes an appropriate note of academic pomp and civic circumstance. The story behind its design is a fascinating one and is well worth telling but there are other buildings and other stories as well.

The architecture of the Queen's campus presents overall a legacy of some distinction and considerable stylistic variety which reflects the changing epochs and academic developments of the last one hundred and fifty years. The buildings of the nineteenth century and the early years of this century maintained the tradition of Gothic revivalism established by the original college but the buildings which immediately preceded, and followed, the Second World War were marked by the prevalent neo-Georgian style of the time. With the large expansion plan of the 1960s came yet more architectural changes which have continued to the present day.

In addition to the buildings commissioned for Queen's through the years, other properties have been acquired and the university campus now comprises over 250 buildings ranging from individual houses to some major complexes. It all amounts to a vast estate, much of it located within the Queen's Conservation Area, the first to be designated in Belfast.

A number of the buildings on the campus are now statutorily listed. Although their qualities have been recognised officially that does not in itself guarantee their future. That can only be achieved with continued care and attention to their fabric, based on a belief in the value of their place in our society. We hope that the following pages will serve that practical objective as well as fulfilling a more academic purpose.

Both as a patron of new architecture through the years, and now as the guardian of a sizeable heritage of historic buildings, as well as some attractive landscapes and gardens, the Queen's University of Belfast has an important role to play in safeguarding our architectural legacy.

1

The Opening of Queen's, and a Royal Occasion

The opening of Queen's College Belfast, on Thursday 20th December 1849 was evidently a particularly splendid Victorian occasion. The assembled guests in the Great Hall included "scarlet robed town councillors, uniformed soldiers and foreign consuls and gaily apparelled ladies", who "presented a pleasing contrast to the sombre gowns of the professors and students and dresses of the gentlemen".[1] As the college president, Dr Henry, rose at noon to address the crowded assembly, a royal salute was fired from the battery on Queen's Island. In his speech the president referred to the new building as a "temple of concord rising in symmetrical and harmonious form." He praised the great statesman Sir Robert Peel, "to whose courage and far seeing wisdom we owe the provincial colleges of Ireland". He also referred to Peel's suggestion some years before that Queen Victoria herself would come to lay the college foundations.

As it turned out, the royal visit came too late for the foundation laying but Queen Victoria and Prince Albert did arrive in Belfast in time to inspect the nearly completed building, some four months before the official opening. Their visit on August 11th is recorded as a great success and the royal couple enjoyed a tumultuous welcome.[2] There were, however, some inauspicious moments: the passage of the royal yacht from Kingstown had been rough and unpleasant and despite a "charming, gracious, expression", "the Queen's features had an air of weariness and showed the effects of sun and wind". She was rather plainly dressed in a robe of blue flounced tabinet and wore no ornament of any kind. Prince Albert in a black body coat, was universally admired for "the noble bearing of his manner and the grace of his movements". The royal party transferred to the steam yacht Fairey in Belfast Lough and arrived at the quay at the end of High Street at about 2 o'clock. Here "in consequence of the tide or some other cause" it was impossible to gain access to the Fairey "without breach of etiquette". That problem solved, after a slight delay, the Queen and her consort received the "principal nobility and gentry" who had assembled since 10 o'clock in the morning.

After disembarking, the Royal couple made their way to the White Linen Hall travelling in the carriage of the Marquis of Londonderry, escorted by a squadron of the 12th Light Dragoons. On their way they passed under a triumphal arch, bearing the friendly greeting 'Ceidh Mile Failte' which had been erected in High Street. The Royal party then drove to the Lisburn Road where "the beauty of the rural scenery began to diversify the route of the procession". The Queen and her consort were able to view the exterior of the workhouse and the Institute for the Deaf and Dumb and Blind. To the disappointment of a large reception committee, including the Bishop of Down and Connor and the principal, who had been waiting on the terrace of the Institute for upwards of an hour, regaled by 'select airs' played by the band of

2

The west front of Queen's as photographed in the late 19th century.

the 7th Guards, the royal procession swept past the Institute and turned left through the grounds of Elmwood House and made for Botanic (now University) Road. The vicinity of the college had been tidied up for the royal visit. Some small houses had been cleared, the ground had been levelled and a neat wall, of the brick used in the college, had been built.[3]

The royal carriage and cavalcade then entered the Botanic Gardens by the newly prepared entrance on the west side and drove through the grounds. Prince Albert it seems discussed horticultural matters with the curator, and the Queen, in a departure from the scheduled programme, expressed to the Mayor her intention to visit the interior of the college, rather than driving past the exterior as had been planned. Somehow, at short notice a reception party was formed and the royal couple were met by the President the Rev. Dr Henry, the Vice-President Dr Andrews, and the architect Charles Lanyon who conducted them through the outer hall and through the examination hall for which they expressed their admiration. Thence they proceeded along the cloisters, facing away from the President's residence, the Queen possibly unaware of the patriotic 'VR 1848' in diapered brickwork which decorates the chimney. Prince Albert, meanwhile, was making intelligent enquiries about the lecture rooms and other apartments. Such was his interest in the college that it was a general desire that he should be its first chancellor when the Queen's University was established in the following year – an honour which he regretfully declined. After signing a royal album, the royal party left the building amid 'deafening cheers'. The unoccupied college was the only building in Belfast where the Queen visited the interior, due to the recent cholera epidemic in the town. The procession then returned to High Street where the royal couple boarded the Fairey and departed at about 6 o'clock. At Her Majesty's order the crew of the Fairey declaimed three cheers from the stern to the acclamation of the crowd.

The Site and the Architect

The Irish Colleges Act, whereby the three colleges at Belfast, Cork, and Galway were established, had made its progress through parliament in 1845 and received Royal Assent on 31st July that year, and on 30th December, Her Majesty ordained "that in or near the town of Belfast, in our province of Ulster, in Ireland shall and may be erected and established a Perpetual College for students of Arts, Law, Physics and other useful learning, which College shall be called by the name Queen's College, Belfast".

The selection of the site was, it seems, a matter of some controversy and there were many different claims. Although Armagh and Londonderry were considered there was no real doubt that the college should be in Belfast where the medical profession was already well established. It was suggested by Sir James Graham, who introduced the Colleges Bill in parliament, that the managers of the Royal Academical Institution might hand over their buildings for the Queen's College, on easy terms. This view was supported by the Rev. Henry Montgomery, leader of the Non-Subscribing Presbyterians who suggested that Sir John Soane's ambitious, but only partially built, scheme for the Institution could be extended upon its original lines. The Rev. Henry Cooke of the orthodox presbyterians opposed this suggestion, however, and denounced "the folly of building a national college on a diminutive site in the midst of factory chimneys".[4] (To this day his statue, at the end of Wellington Place, known locally as the black man, turns his face against the 'Inst' site). Cooke advocated the site adjoining the Botanic Gardens, the property of Miss Gregg and known as 'The Plains', which could extend from the Malone Road as far as the River Lagan. The architect Charles Lanyon also opposed the Institution site, maintaining that buildings on it would require piling, and consequently buildings on another site would be less expensive, and besides, "the severely utilitarian character of the Institute"[5] evidently did not appeal to him.

Lanyon (1813–1889) was the most prominent architect in Ulster at this time. An Englishman by birth, he had trained in Dublin with Jacob Owen, the

Portrait of Charles Lanyon (1813–1889).

architect of the Office of Public Works in Ireland, before being appointed County Surveyor of Antrim and moving to Belfast. Among his most important achievements locally were the Courthouse and Gaol, the Custom House, Queen's Bridge and Ormeau Bridge, the Palm House in Botanic Gardens, the Presbyterian College in Botanic Avenue, and the Institute for the Deaf and Dumb and Blind on Lisburn Road, most of which dated from the 1840s to 50s. Later he became, in turn, Mayor of Belfast and Conservative MP for Belfast, and he was knighted in 1868. A remarkable man and the most important architect of his generation in Ireland, he retired from practice in 1872 and died in 1889.

Under the Colleges Act the Commissioners of Public Works were empowered to employ "the county surveyor, or any other competent surveyor or architect" to draw up plans, specifications and estimates. In the case of Belfast, Charles Lanyon was not only county surveyor, and a very competent architect, but was also the son-in-law of Jacob Owen, the architect to the Commissioners.

In January 1846 Charles Lanyon not surprisingly was appointed the architect for the college, and the site beside the Botanic Gardens was chosen. The selection of this site marked the acceleration of the growth of the town in a southerly direction, and the migration from the estuarial plains, or slob lands, of the old town towards the undulating and well drained Malone ridge, later characterised as "the snob lands of south Belfast".[6] The process was already under way: the Botanic Gardens had been established in 1827 and the development of what is now the site of the Belfast City Hospital included the Institute for the Deaf and Dumb and Blind (1845), the Union Workhouse (1841) and the Fever Hospital (1845). The arrival of Queen's was soon followed by colleges for the Presbyterians (1853) and the Methodists (1868). Congregations which had been established in the old town were drawn to the attractions of the academic milieu and an array of Gothic revival churches soon began to steeple the south Belfast skyline. In the 1920s the Belfast Museum's move to the Botanic Gardens was a further consolidation of the status of the area.

The selected site, some ten acres in area, was acquired by the Board of Works, and the lowest tender, by the builder Cranston Gregg, was accepted and the contract signed on June 23rd 1847. The three new Irish colleges in Belfast, Cork, and Galway were to share equally the funds of £100,000 and a

Ground plan of the original college building, as designed by Charles Lanyon (from the Board of Works' report of 1848).

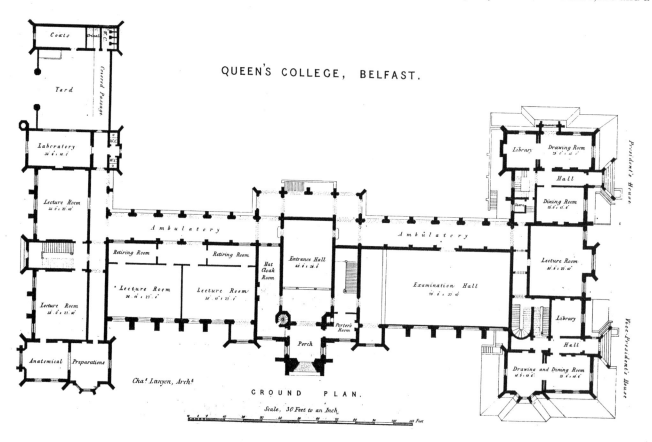

QUEEN'S COLLEGE, BELFAST.

GROUND PLAN.

Scale, 30 Feet to an Inch.

6

Lanyon's design of 1847 for the west front. The draughtsmanship on this drawing was the work of his young apprentice W.H. Lynn.

general scheme of accommodation had been prescribed. As the colleges were non-denominational there was no provision for a chapel which gave rise to the term 'Godless colleges'. The schedule consisted of a great hall for public purposes, a library, a museum of natural history, a chemical laboratory and an apparatus room for physics and mechanics; six lecture rooms, each with a seating capacity of 200; a room for professors; a students' cloakroom; a cloister for exercise in wet weather and residences for the President and Vice-President. Lanyon's scheme departed slightly from this prescription and provided eight lecture rooms of varying sizes. When Cranston Gregg's tender was opened however, it had been found to be thirty percent over budget. This must have been a severe blow to Lanyon who, with economy very much in mind, had chosen to use brickwork, the other Irish colleges being built of stone. The Board of Works required economies to be made and the subsequent pruning exercise removed many of the details that had been indicated on the original contract drawings of 1847, such as fantastic Elizabethan-style chimney pots, roof lanterns (described as 'lanthorns' in the drawings), canopied niches flanking the top window of the tower, stone screens across the entrance hall and the great hall, as well as a gallery in the great hall.

At an earlier stage a major item of accommodation had also been omitted. That was the examination hall as originally projected. It was intended to have stood on axis with the main entrance tower and to have been elevated to first floor level and approached by a great staircase leading from the entrance hall. The loss of this grandiose scheme (suggesting processions of robed

7

QUEEN'S COLLEGE, BELFAST.

Published by W^m McComb 1 High St Belfast.

A contemporary engraving showing the Queen's College.

A view in the quadrangle, showing the eastern elevation of the Lanyon Building. Photographed in 1949 before changes to the north wing.

Entrance Hall.

Elevation of Door and Window above Landing of principal Staircase.

Plan.

Lanyon's original drawing of 1847 for the large traceried window in the east wall of the entrance hall. Neither the central doorway shown here, intended to lead to an examination hall planned for the centre of the quadrangle, nor the first floor landing referred to on the drawing, were built. As finally erected the tracery of the large window was less elaborate than shown here.

Lanyon's drawing of 1847 for the main entrance tower on the west front.

academics making their ceremonial way through the entrance hall and ascending the stairs to the hall) has deprived the entrance hall as it is now, of a sense of focus and direction. On the other hand the proposed examination hall would have been a major encroachment upon the present spacious lawns of the quadrangle and the effect of the great traceried east window, which now lights the entrance hall, would be less dramatic.

The omission of the proposed examination hall from Lanyon's original scheme of 1846 was to prove a short term economy, however, as within months of the opening of the college it was found necessary to double the size of the museum, and the library was forced to share the accommodation of the examination hall. As student numbers grew the shared use of the space became almost unworkable and the need for a new library became acute.

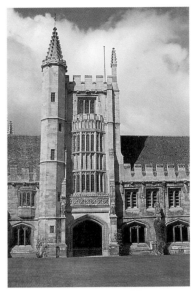

The Founder's tower at Magdalen College, Oxford, dating from 1474; a Tudor model used by many Victorian architects for collegiate buildings.

The Lanyon Building

The revival of historic styles was more than an exercise in nostalgia for the Victorians. It was a kind of erudite game of symbol and reference. Quotations of historic precedent were used to establish a building's authority and pedigree and for academic lineage the late Gothic and Tudor styles of the Oxbridge colleges were the ideal source. These buildings employ the pointed arch, but usually in a flattened form, as well as square headed windows with mullions and transoms. To meet the demands of this historicist approach to design came the publication of pattern books recording the detail of the great mediaeval buildings and publishing measured drawings and surveys. There is no doubt that Lanyon copied the whole gateway tower of Magdalen College in Oxford fairly closely in designing the central tower of Queen's. It is not a replica in the narrow sense of the word, Lanyon's version being taller and narrower in proportion, and built of brick. Furthermore, Moody and Beckett suggest that "each portion of the west façade (of Queen's), to left and right of the cross gables is an adaptation of the late mediaeval college chapel such as that at Magdalen."[7]

It has been pointed out that Lanyon's design has some affinities with Trinity College at Glenalmond in Perthshire by the Edinburgh architect James Henderson, which opened in 1834.[8] Trinity College has a central tower which was also modelled on the Founder's Tower at Magdalen College and it is very similar to that of Queen's. It also has two flanking towers near the ends of the front façade, but these are not given the same importance as those at Queen's and the overall composition seems less decisive, lacking the same contrast between solid and largely glazed areas.

The Illustrated London News of 8th February, 1851, shows a good engraving of the Queen's College, Belfast, as built, and a brief description. Other

A detail of a bay window to one of the end towers of the west front of Queen's.

An original perspective drawing for the Queen's College. In this version of the design, dating from 1846, the octagonal stair turret appears at the front of the main entrance tower.

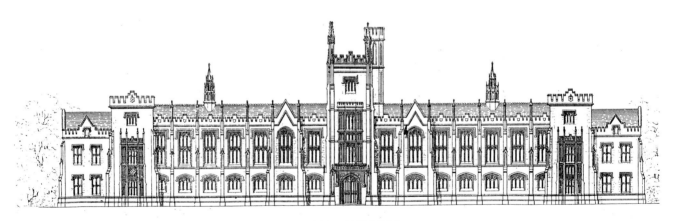

FRONT ELEVATION.

Elevational drawing for the west front, as published in the report of the Board of Works in 1848. In this version the stair turret is to the rear of the main tower and is shown to the right of the entrance.

contemporary issues of that publication also featured several newly built colleges which show a similar design ancestry to Queen's.

Architects of this period in the British Isles, following the completion of the Houses of Parliament by Barry and Pugin, saw English Tudor as the national style as well as the embodiment of learning and piety. The other Irish Colleges at Galway and Cork also followed the trend. Lanyon may have had in mind his own Institute for the Deaf and Dumb and Blind (completed 1845), which presented a long symmetrical façade to the Lisburn Road across an expanse of lawns. Lanyon was a classicist by nature and training and he may have admired (despite his opinion of its architectural character) the symmetry and siting of the Academical Institution in Belfast, with the axial approach then bisecting the open space in front. One may surmise that Lanyon's instinct for symmetry presented him with a design dilemma because the Founder's Tower with its corner turret is decidedly asymmetrical, but historical authenticity required the presence of a turret in any design based on the original. This may explain the indecision as to the position of the turret at Queen's. The perspective drawing of the first version in 1846 shows it prominently on the front of the tower, and in the drawings published by the Board of Works in their report of 1848, it is shown to the rear right of the tower on the elevation, although on the plans it appears on the rear left. The authors offer the thought here that its eventual position in the shade of the rear north side of the tower was chosen as being the most inconspicuous location.

Whatever its pedigree, Lanyon's west front is the enduring image of Queen's. It has all the virtues of the best Victorian architecture, bold massing, a memorable silhouette and plenty of architectural detail. It is eminently Victorian too in striking an appropriate note of academic pomp and civic circumstance. The long façade is a masterly interplay of progressions and recessions, and the balance between vertical and horizontal lines. The sequence of rectangular traceried windows to left and right of the tower is interrupted by two projecting cross gables which introduce the diagonal to the design and serve as visual reinforcements to the tower. It may not be coincidence that an equilateral triangle lines up both gables with the tops of the pinnacles on the tower – this kind of geometrical device as an aid to composition would certainly have been familiar to an architect like Lanyon. The corner towers are stumpy restatements of the theme of the central tower with similar canted bay windows rising from ground level. They act as book-ends to the long façade and make for an easy change of scale as both wings of the building turn east.

The design has not been without its critics,[9] however, particularly later generations of architects concerned with the niceties of expressing the interior function of a building in the form of the exterior. The single volume of the Great Hall, it has been pointed out, reads exactly the same as the lecture

The main entrance tower to Queen's as eventually built, with the stair turret appearing to the rear left.

A bay window to one of the end towers of the west front.

13

A quatrefoil ventilating panel below one of the large windows on the west front.

A detail of the top of the octagonal stair turret to the main entrance tower.

rooms and library, which occupied two storeys to the left of the main tower. It has been observed that "the red brick Tudor façade cloaked a façade as classical as Barry's at Westminster Palace a decade earlier".[10]

A more pressing concern was the heating and ventilation of the building. The original drawings show a natural ventilation system of the kind that was fairly common practice at the time, particularly in the design of ecclesiastical buildings and one with which Lanyon was well acquainted. Solid exterior walls were built with an interior lining of lath and plaster, with a cavity between. It was important that this cavity be ventilated and internal and external grills were used. At Queen's these occur at regular intervals on the façade, particularly below window openings and are expressed as quatrefoil carved sandstone openings. This system meant that rooms could be provided with some natural ventilation without having to open the windows, something of a problem with large cast-iron diamond-paned lights. Lanyon was also concerned with ventilating the science block at the north end of the building and the internal ventilation grills connect with separate flues in the chimney stacks; the drawings show the system in colour coding. Gases were extracted from the chemistry laboratory by the octagonal turret that terminates the north east extremity of the original college.

Heating of the building was a more thorny problem. At the official opening the crowded Great Hall was unheated and the college had to wait until March 1850 for a permanent system to be installed and even then it was not in working order during the first session. It was a hot air system operated by a central furnace and steam engine constructed by William Walker of Manchester. (This was presumably situated in the basements beneath the residences of the President and Vice-President). Even when functioning perfectly it could not heat both the lecture room and the examination hall and the Council decided to install patent self-feeding stoves provided by Messrs Riddell of Belfast – these must have placed a severe strain upon the natural ventilation!

The architects of the other two Irish colleges, J.B. Keane at Galway and Thomas Deane at Cork, opted for quadrangular plans and both colleges were built of stone. As both the plan form and the choice of material were hardly the least expensive option, and both colleges were built on cost to the specifications of the Board of Works, the thought occurs that the pound, at that time, bought more in Cork and Galway than Belfast. The Great Famine was then at its height and the tragedy was more keenly felt in Connaught and Munster than Ulster, circumstances which may have had a bearing upon the price of building work. Lanyon's approach, partly with economy in mind was to present one great façade to University Road and to lay out the plan of the building in the configuration of the letter 'E'. (As originally projected the central examination hall would have represented the middle horizontal line of the E and the north and south wings the top and bottom). The precedent

14

was the great Elizabethan country houses laid out as an 'E' in honour of the Queen. The symbolic associations between that 'Golden Age' and the ambitions of Victorian Ulster are clearly spelt out.

The choice of plan may have been occasioned by Lanyon's awareness of the likelihood of future expansion which would give succeeding architects a freer hand at developing the scheme. Lanyon used bricks manufactured on the college site (laid to the English practice of four courses per twelve inches rather than the more generous Irish dimensions) and sandstone dressings from Scrabo in Co. Down. He lavished much of his budget on the west front and the two wings at each end, using an assortment of 'specimens' of Gothic detailing with compositional assurance.

For all their belief in Utopian progress the Victorians had a deep and lasting love of the past and a particular fascination with the mediaeval world, its architecture and its pageantry as recalled in the romantic novels of Sir Walter Scott. This 'retrophilia' as it has been called, accounts for much of Victorian architecture and at Queen's the savage strangeness of mediaeval carvings is revived in the fantastic gargoyle heads which decorate the turret of the main tower. These grimacing faces with open mouths ready to cascade rain-water hardly agree with our ideas of Victorian sensibility. Elsewhere in the college other enigmatic faces such as those flanking the main entrance door gaze out and their identity remains unknown, as too, until recently were the names of the masons who had carved them.

In a letter to the University in 1994 Professor Symmers of North Carolina reported that documents in Australia had established that the Master Mason for the Lanyon Building was his great grandfather (on his mother's side), Robert McCredie. McCredie did not live to complete the work, as he died in 1848, but his five sons, one of whom succeeded him as Master Mason, carried out the contract before emigrating to Australia. Professor Symmers, the source of this information, grew up in Belfast where his father was Professor of Pathology at Queen's from 1904 to 1929.

The south wing, smaller in scale than the west façade, as befits the largely domestic accommodation, does not lack architectural incident; notably the entrance doors to the former presidential residences. Miniature flying buttresses act as handrails, buttressing only the unsteady visitor. The north wing lacks these architectural conceits but the entrance doorway presents another pair of mysterious carved heads. The eastern façade was austere in comparison, and presented blank walls above the cloisters, the library, museum and examination hall being lit from the west side only. A single storey was added above the south cloister by J.H. Owen in 1863–5 and a two storey addition was built above the north cloister to designs by Dr Robert Cochrane in 1904–5. These additions, though asymmetrical, have added variety to the elevation.

The Great Hall, the major architectural event of the interior also reveals

Above and below: two carved sandstone heads at the doorway to the north wing of the Lanyon Building. Their identities have not been recorded, but it is likely that they represent pioneers in the fields of science and medicine.

15

Interior of the Great Hall showing its fine Gothic queen-post roof; photographed in 1949.

signs of parsimony. A near contemporary account by J.B. Doyle in *Tours of Ulster*, published in 1854, describes it as 'raw and unpoetic' despite the grandeur of scale. Fitted out as the college library, as was originally conceived, and lined with books and galleries, it would have been a memorable space. Today it is used as a dining hall and for occasional academic functions. Above the handsome stone fireplace hangs a copy of Titian's 'St Peter the Martyr' by James Atkins, which was presented to the college in 1847. The panelled walls are hung with portraits of distinguished academics of the past and the great hammer-beam roof is decorated with ten carved angels resembling figure heads on sailing ships, bearing shields on each alternate one of which is emblazoned the arms of Ulster.

The entrance hall is much enhanced by the great stained glass window at the east end. It was designed by J.E. Nuttgens in 1939 but was not erected until after the war. Its inscription reads as follows: "This window is dedicated to the memory of all Queensmen and Queenswomen who having served their generation have fallen on sleep. Their epitaph is graven not on stone but on the hearts of men." The college had to wait almost a hundred years for this addition – at the time of the official opening the window was unglazed. The handsome commemorative bronze plaque to the president Thomas Hamilton

The stained glass memorial window in the entrance hall of the Lanyon Building. Designed by J.E. Nuttgens in 1939 but not erected until after the Second World War.

18

was erected almost half a century before in 1907. He had, the citation reads, "justly earned the gratitude of posterity and the enduring reputation of a second founder." The extraordinary and elongated painting of St Patrick, hidden away behind an arch above a small staircase on the south side of the hall, is a surprise and a somewhat incongruous feature. It was carried out by students of the Belfast College of Art in the 1950s.

Canada Room, Council Chamber and Visitors' Centre

As Queen's expanded over the years, the range to the north of the tower was taken over by administration and the old lecture rooms and museum were partitioned for office space. After the move to the new administration building in 1975 a major improvement scheme was carried out by the architect Robert McKinstry to accommodate a new council chamber and a reception room known as the Canada Room, both of which opened in 1986. The project has given back to the interior of this part of the building something approaching its original spatial quality. The Council Chamber rises the full two storey height of the old Museum to reveal Lanyon's roof trusses, and a new gallery, very much along the lines indicated in the original drawings, runs along the east side. The single storey Canada Room is situated below a new seminar room and suite of offices for the Vice-Chancellor. A new return flight of stairs leads off the entrance hall to the Canada Room, and McKinstry has reused the carved balustrade and newel posts which formerly belonged to the staircase at the other side of the entrance hall, and for the half landing he commissioned a mural by Cherith McKinstry portraying a delightfully dreamlike vision of student life.

Lanyon's heraldic marble newel post with balustraded stairway, in its new location to the north of the entrance hall.

Much of Lanyon's interior decor harks back to an earlier phase of the Gothic revival, sometimes referred to as 'Gentleman's Gothic', in which simple pointed forms are handled with an almost Georgian delicacy. The surviving staircase in the former President's residence is a good example of Lanyon's pared-down Tudor detailing.

McKinstry, who like W.A. Forsyth, has worked for the National Trust, is noted for his building conservation work, particularly for the restoration of the Grand Opera House, Belfast. At Queen's his handling of the restoration has admirably caught the feel of Lanyon's original decor, sympathetically respecting the old yet belonging unmistakably to the present. The tall door opening, with its tripartite fanlight and chamfered surrounds, which leads into the Canada Room is an excellent instance. The conversion of part of the ground floor range beneath the Canada Room for use as a visitors' centre (known as the Lanyon Room), by the Belfast firm of architects, Twenty Two Over Seven, likewise respects the old college without sacrificing any of its own personality. It was opened in 1995.

The staircase of the former President's residence in the south wing.

The library as originally built to the designs of Lanyon, Lynn and Lanyon, 1865–8.

The Old Library

In 1865 the government agreed to fund a new library and the Board of Works appointed the firm of Lanyon, Lynn and Lanyon as architects. Charles Lanyon was by now in partnership with both his young assistant who had worked on the drawings of the original college and acted as Clerk of Works for it, and his own son John. The building, a separate block rather than the extension to the east wing proposed by the Board of Works, was to have been situated alongside University Square, roughly facing the present Whitla Hall. The acquisition of the houses, including Botanic Cottage which then occupied the site, presented some difficulties and the library was eventually situated closer to the main building allowing for possible future expansion to either east or west.

This new building (now popularly known as the Old Library) resembled the nave of a church and was designed by Lanyon's partner William Henry Lynn. In an article in the student magazine *Gown* in 1984, the poet Philip Larkin, who was sub-librarian at Queen's from 1950–55, recalled with pleasure his time there, and wrote of his having enjoyed working in the building which resembled, as he put it, "a large church designed by an ecclesiastical architect".[11] Perhaps Lynn had indeed intended to give the 'Godless College' at least the appearance of possessing a chapel. The high pitched gable with its great traceried window echoes the form of the twin cross gables that frame the central tower of the Lanyon Building. The library is an admirable companion piece to the old college despite the dramatic changes in architectural thinking which marked the intervening twenty years. The High Victorian phase of architecture, roughly coinciding with the third quarter of the nineteenth century, was inspired to a large degree by the vociferous art critic John Ruskin. Ruskin advocated the eclectic mixture of styles encompassing Continental Gothic as well as English and favoured the use of a wide palette of colours and materials together with an abundance of naturalistic carvings – Lynn was one of his most fervent admirers in Ireland. Building of the library began in 1866 and was completed in 1868.

Lynn's later extension to the library in 1911 was admirably executed. In his recommendations to the university, Sir Aston Webb had suggested that the library should be joined to the main buildings by building two link blocks but Lynn's solution was simply to extend the building to the west, without apparent join, and fuse old and new almost invisibly by maintaining the Ruskinian detailing throughout. Stylistically, Lynn's treatment was very anachronistic, yet it produced a very satisfactory result. The join of the old library with its extension is marked by a roof lantern and by the slight mis-match of the colouring of the banded roof slates. Until the later insertion of a floor at gallery level, the High Victorian interior of the library was one of Ireland's richest. "With its high roof and great west window beneath which, in winter,

A detail of the Old Library showing a carved stone gargoyle.

Engraved view of the interior of the Old Library in the 1870s.

Opposite page: west gable of the Old Library. The building was originally opened in 1868 and extended to the west in 1911.

A detail of the Old Library, showing the roof ventilator and some of the polychrome brick and stonework.

A detail of the Old Library.

A portrait photograph of W.H. Lynn (1829–1915).

a huge fire blazed in an open grate, . . . it seemed the ideal of a library reading room," according to Moody and Beckett.[12] At first floor level much of the quality of the building has survived, even allowing for the insertion of the new intermediate floor by John MacGeagh in 1952 and the later addition of a new staircase and glass vaulted mezzanine for the rare books collection (sensitively carried out by Twist and Whitley in 1983). Beneath the diagonally boarded ceiling, Ruskinian detail abounds; polychrome arches spring from piers decorated with multi-coloured marble shafts and capitals of carved stone foliage glimmer in the light of plate traceried windows and stained glass.

Although John MacGeagh added some new windows at ground floor level when the intermediate floor was built in 1952 (their position identifiable by the presence of plain block capitals to columns rather than carvings) and he also inserted a new door on the University Square elevation, the exterior of the Old Library has largely survived intact. It blends successfully with the original Lanyon building and makes a strong statement of its own, characterised by its brick and polychrome stonework, gables and gargoyles and interesting silhouette.

The 1910 Extension Scheme

In 1908 Queen's College was created a full University, having become a constituent part of the Royal University of Ireland in 1881. The treasury then agreed to a major programme of building work to extend the facilities. This included extensions to the Library, the Students' Union, and the medical block, a new science block (now the Old Physics building), and a Drill Hall for the Officers Training Corps.

In February 1910, Sir Aston Webb, the President of the Royal Institute of British Architects visited Belfast to advise on the development of the University and among his recommendations was the insertion of a new floor in the Library at the level of the galleries, the new upper storey to become a reading room, and the space below to be used for storage. This was a proposal that had to wait until 1952 for its realisation. The other suggestions in 1910, such as the siting of new buildings on the front lawn, were never taken up.

The Senate's Building Committee had taken over responsibility for the development of Queen's from the Board of Works, and in 1910 announced its decision to hold an open competition for the works. Fifty seven designs were received, submitted anonymously, the authors' names being enclosed in separate envelopes. When the selection was made the adjudicator Sir Aston Webb declared the winning entry to be by the eighty-two-year-old William Henry Lynn.

A view of the south wing of Queen's main building showing, to the left, one of Lanyon's entrance porches with its unusual 'flying buttress' handrails; to the right, W.H. Lynn's Old Physics tower erected in 1911; and in the centre, the link block inserted by W.A. Forsyth in 1933–4.

It is tempting to wonder just how 'anonymous' an entry such as Lynn's might have been. His ability as a draughtsman and watercolourist was widely acclaimed, and he had established a national and international reputation as an architect with competition-winning entries for buildings throughout the British Isles and as far afield as Sydney, and commissions from Quebec to Constantinople. In 1867 he achieved the singular distinction of winning the architecture Gold Medal at the Paris International exhibition. However, as recorded by Lynn's colleague Kyle Knox, it was characteristic of him that "not content with the conditions of the competition he left Belfast before the various designs were exhibited to avoid the possibility of even meeting the assessor".[13] Knox was the chairman of the Building Committee at Queen's and it fell to him to announce to the Senate the selection of the designs of W.H. Lynn; there was, he writes "loud applause and manifest pleasure". Knox had recently been presented with the original drawings of the college by the chairman of the Board of Works in Dublin; these included an elevation of the west front "showing in minute detail all the ornamental work of the Great Tower and the entire façade". As Knox recalled, "I could not refrain from expressing to Mr Lynn, who stood behind my chair, my regret at seeing this beautiful piece of work spoiled by neglect. "Well", said he "Knox, I could

25

not do it now but that is my work. I drew it in 1846. That is to say 64 years before."

The University later acknowledged a lifetime's service by this great architect: in the former south entrance porch of the Library is a wall mounted commemorative plaque to W.H. Lynn with an inscription which reads:

This tablet is erected by his friends in memory of William Henry Lynn RHA an architect whose name and works are known and admired not alone in England, Ireland and Scotland but in the most distant parts of the empire. This is also a record of the fact that the original college buildings erected in 1846, which owed much to his professional skill were by his designs completed in 1913 on an extended scale for the new University of Belfast in the 85th year of his age.

In his report on the competition, Webb, the assessor who had also prepared the conditions, characterised Lynn's design "as a very masterly one and the best submitted in the competition".[14] Lynn's most daring proposal was to provide a large central museum hall immediately to the rear of the entrance hall, spanning almost the entire width of the quadrangle and enclosed on the east side by the Natural Science departments. Lynn claimed this would "avoid blocking up ground towards the front of the present building that would be better left open, while it occupies ground in the quadrangle that is otherwise useless and in doing so reduces the quadrangle to more reasonable dimensions".[15] The top-lit museum hall, approached through the main entrance hall would have been a spectacular architectural event but the scheme was never realised. Lynn's opinion of the merits of the quad make for strange reading; it is a well loved feature of the campus and few today would regard its dimensions as unreasonable nor any of its space as useless. Lynn's scheme, however, unlike both the second and third placed entries in the competition, did enclose the south side of the quad and provided a coherent if somewhat reduced space.

This south range which now houses the Physics department is dominated by the tower, with archway beneath, a companion piece to Lanyon's great tower, and replete with its own octagonal turret. It is economically designed in a restrained Tudor style in red brick with sandstone dressings. The tower boldly announces the cross axis of the pathway which bisects the quad at the change of level. (A modest response to Lynn's tower was later added to the northern range by John MacGeagh in 1952). Twin staircases rise from the archway giving access to the lecture theatre and a coat of arms on the quadrangle side bears the inscription 'RUI 1881' recording the creation of the Royal University of Ireland. This shield was carved by Morris Harding as recently as 1948 as were the carved corbels to the springing of the vaults in the archway. These feature shamrocks, leeks, thistles and roses, denoting the four home countries.

A shield on the north face of the Old Physics tower depicting the arms of the Royal University of Ireland which was created in 1881; carved by Morris Harding in 1948.

The Old Physics tower built in 1911 to the designs of W.H. Lynn. Its square plan, Tudor archway, and octagonal stair turret echo Lanyon's earlier tower on the west front of the college.

A view looking north through the archways of the Old Physics tower and the north tower, with a fanlit door on University Square in the distance.

The south wing was not completed to Lynn's original design, and for some years there existed between the tower and the former President's residence a small gap which was not bridged until 1933–34 by W.A. Forsyth. This building which finally completed the southern range of the quadrangle, was known as the Arts Building and it houses, at ground floor level, the Senate Room. It was built in rustic brick with stone dressings and links admirably the works of Charles Lanyon and William Henry Lynn.

Above: a corbel in the archway of the Old Physics tower carved with shamrocks to represent Ireland, as one of a 'Commonwealth series', by Morris Harding, 1948.

The Music Department

From the 1860s onwards the quadrangle had been gradually enclosed along the northern and eastern boundaries by a heterogeneous collection of buildings which included the Schools of Medicine and Chemistry. Of the surviving buildings the present School of Music is the most notable. Designed as the Students' Union by Dr Robert Cochrane of the Board of Works, the foundation stone was laid on the 18th of January 1896 by the Lord Lieutenant of Ireland, Earl Cadogan. The building in red brick with stone dressings follows the Tudor style of the main college. The interior includes a generous staircase with stained glass to its mullioned window, timber panelling and a galleried hall. It was almost imperceptibly extended by W.H. Lynn in 1911–13 who

Below: a view of the former Students' Union (now the Music Department) as originally built to the designs of Robert Cochrane in 1896.

29

The dining room of the former Students' Union (now the Harty Room), built to the designs of W.A. Forsyth in 1932–3. Only oak pins, rather than iron bolts or screws, were used in the construction of the hammer-beam roof.

The Harty Room of the Music Department, originally the dining room of the old Students' Union.

added the copper cupola. In 1932–3 a dining hall was added by W.A. Forsyth from London, who had designed a wide range of educational buildings including Hull University College and work on Eton and Harrow and was also a consultant architect for the National Trust. It was opened by Mr Stanley Baldwin, chairman of the Pilgrim Trust which donated the money to build it. This dining hall (now the Harty Room of the Department of Music) has one of the finest hammer-beam roofs in Ireland, and is a distinguished addition to the campus. It was the last major piece of architecture at Queen's to respect and honour the style of the old college building, while its form echoes the steeply pitched roof of the old library with which it is aligned.

The Sir William Whitla Hall

The Sir William Whitla Hall was the most notable 20th century addition to the main campus. It was originally designed in 1936[16] and started in 1939 just before the Second World War, but was not completed until after the war, in 1949. A large free-standing assembly hall – made possible by a bequest of Sir William Whitla, formerly Professor of Materia Medica, who died in 1933 – it was the work of John MacGeagh, a rising young Belfast architect who had attracted the attention of the then Vice-Chancellor Dr Frederick Ogilvie, a man whose principal interest outside his academic work was art. As the commission amounted to a considerable responsibility for a young architect, MacGeagh was allowed to appoint a consultant. His choice was Edward Maufe of London.

Built of hand-made rough-surfaced facing bricks from Buckley in Lancashire, with Clipsham stone used for surrounds to windows, doors and other dressings, the flat-roofed blocky form of the hall sits serenely overlooking the front lawn of the main building. At the time the juxtaposition of the simple modern design with the Lanyon building caused a certain amount of controversy. It was apparently Ogilvie, as much as anyone, who decided that there would be no attempt to follow the Tudor Gothic pattern already set at Queen's. The Whitla Hall was the first building at the university to break with that Tudor revivalist tradition, but as has been observed by Moody and Beckett "this deliberate contrast, somewhat modified by the use of red brick and by the comparative isolation of the new building, is far more satisfying than any merely imitative design could probably have been".[17] The new building has mellowed so much that few people, if any, would argue today with the contrast, and in any case, although seen as frankly modern at the time, MacGeagh's design displayed a leaning towards the serenity of the Georgian period, and so, in a subtle way it has always acknowledged the general

The entrance front of the Sir William Whitla Hall. Designed in the 1930s by John MacGeagh but not completed until after the Second World War.

A view of the west side of the Whitla Hall.

Above: a keystone on the west side of the Whitla Hall, depicting an owl.

Georgian character of much of the district around the university, particularly the terrace of University Square which faces it across the lawn.

The rectangular forms of the Whitla Hall grow logically out of the plan, the low blocks at each side of the main entrance giving scale to the mass of the hall behind, this in turn being broken by the projecting block of the vestibule and the set-back of the clerestoreys above the main cornice. Skilful use was made of sculpture which is well set off by the broad surfaces of the finely textured brickwork. Over the central window of the entrance front there is a carved relief designed by Gilbert Bayes, a distinguished academic sculptor from London, and executed by Morris Harding in 1941. It shows the arms of the university carried on a globe whose supporters, Aesculapius the god of medicine, and a scribe, symbolise the benefactor's twin services to healing and to learning.

Whitla himself is represented by a bronze bust set in a stone niche above the foundation stone as a central feature of the long west wall. The bust was the work of Bayes, while the wreath surrounding it was carved by Harding and the lettering of the foundation stone was by Eric Munday. Morris Harding was also responsible for the execution of Bayes' designs for the carved keystones to the long hall windows, those along the west wall featuring emblems representing the principal faculties of the university and those on the east side identifying the seven chief industries of Northern Ireland at the time. These keystones were all carved *in situ* during 1948.

Below: a keystone on the east side of the Whitla Hall, representing 'aeroplane construction'.

Below: the 'Universal Knowledge' panel over the main entrance to the Whitla Hall.

The vestibule of the Whitla Hall.

Bust of Sir William Whitla by Gilbert Bayes, on the west wall of the Whitla Hall.

Following the laying of its foundation stone on 8th July 1939 by the Marquis of Londonderry the shell of the Whitla Hall, its outer walls and roof, had reached a fairly advanced state by 1942 when war-time restrictions stopped work. The uncompleted hall was requisitioned by the Ministry of Commerce and was used by American troops during the war years, but as MacGeagh acknowledged afterwards, "I cannot praise too highly their care of the building . . . they did not over-load the structure with weights for which the buildings were not designed, and they did not put a single mark on the walls".[18] During those war years the old English oak which had been selected for floors and doors and window casements lay in a supplier's stockyard in Bedford while German bombs wrought destruction all around it, but the wood remained untouched. "We lived in daily fear that all our timber would go up in smoke",[19] recalled MacGeagh who visited the storage site several times during the war. It was not until 1945 that a permit was obtained to proceed with the completion of the interior. When work was restarted progress was slow due mainly to the lack of materials, but finally in 1949 the building was officially opened. The formal ceremony was performed on the 19th February by the eminent scientist and Nobel Prizewinner, Sir Henry Hallet Dare. The bust of Sir William Whitla on the west wall was unveiled before the official opening but there was a slight hitch in the proceedings, when, as the press described,

Sir Henry pulled gently but firmly at the tape. The linen covering stayed fast. He pulled again. Three times he pulled. The Vice-Chancellor looked encouraging. The members of the Belfast Corporation looked a little stern. Here and there scholarly lips twitched in an involuntary grin. Sir Henry pulled again, but there was no heart in the pull. Silently it was agreed to take the gesture for fact and Sir Henry and the Vice-Chancellor, the Councillors Professors and lecturers moved away, solemn and dignified to open the door at the other side of the building. Scarcely had the procession turned the corner than Morris Harding dashed forward with a ladder which one guessed had been placed conveniently for just such an emergency. Two seconds later the bust was unveiled.

The opening of the hall itself revealed an interior of very fine quality. The floors of the vestibules were finished with a combination of Belgian Black and Travertine marble, while the main hall itself was characterised by its woodwork of oak painted silver grey and handrails and balustrading of wrought iron and bronze with the letter 'W' for Whitla worked into them. "The noblest and most dignified building dedicated to the life and studies of Queen's University since Sir Charles Lanyon's work reached completion just a hundred years ago" was how the new Vice-Chancellor Sir David Keir described the hall at the time.[20]

A fitting memorial to a great Queensman, and the masterpiece of its architect John MacGeagh, the patient efforts of over a decade were further rewarded when the Whitla Hall was awarded the RIBA Ulster Architecture Medal for 1950.

Later Additions To The Main Site

John MacGeagh also designed other prominent additions to the main site. Adjacent to the Whitla Hall is his New Physics Building which occupies most of the space to the south of the old Physics building to which it is joined by a curved corridor. Designed as early as 1955, it was erected from 1958 on, and was formally opened on 6th April 1962 by the Queen Mother on her first return to the University since her original visit nearly forty years before to receive an honorary degree. The building's blocky forms in rustic brick and Clipsham stone reflect those of the Whitla Hall but owing to cost restrictions there was no attempt to match the sculptural embellishments which so characterise its illustrious neighbour. Although it is a large building it sits comfortably on its site and recedes quietly into the background. Its most distinguished feature is the entrance tower, judiciously placed facing the old Physics tower and containing a memorable spiral staircase in reinforced concrete.

Entrance tower of the New Physics Building.

Stairway in the entrance tower of the New Physics Building, designed by John MacGeagh in 1955.

On the same axis as the two Physics towers is the one marking the end of the former Engineering Building which MacGeagh added to Lanyon's north wing. Its design dates from 1951, with the first floor oriel added when MacGeagh tidied up the east wall in 1963.

Other MacGeagh works on the main site include the new main entrance gateway of the university, erected in 1949, and the Main Library tower block of 1962–7 which is perhaps not a fair reflection of the architect's ability. MacGeagh was an architect of hand-made rustic brickwork and stone dressings handled in a traditional way, rather than multi-storey framed construction with infill panels.

Another late addition of note to the main campus is the Social Sciences Building erected on the site of the old Chemistry, Bio-Chemistry and Physiology building. It was designed in a modern style by Ulster Architects Partnership in 1962, Donald Shanks being the partner in charge, and was opened by Her Majesty the Queen on 5th July 1966. It was much admired at the time for its attempt to harmonise with but not emulate, the varying Victorian Gothic styles of architecture found in the earlier buildings around it, and received a commendation from the Civic Trust in 1966. "This substan-

The architects' original perspective drawing for the Social Sciences Building, designed in 1962 by Ulster Architects Partnership and opened in 1966. To the left is John MacGeagh's north tower of 1951 and in the background is his library tower of 1962–7.

tial and distinguished building achieves very high standards in general scale, choice of materials, textures and elevational treatment generally" commented the assessor, but despite its commendable design qualities it was adjudged to be just "a wee bit ill at ease"[21] as far as the rest of the existing quadrangle was concerned, mainly as a result of its uncompromising rectangularity. The decision not to link it with the existing north tower in order to avoid a narrow corridor between it and the proposed library extension on the north side, was taken by the architects and the consultant architect at that time, Hugh Casson.

The enclosure of the quadrangle as we see it today was completed in 1975 with the arrival of the new Administration building, designed in 1971 by Cruickshank and Seward. The façade with horizontal bands of red brick and glass links the Social Sciences and Old Physics buildings. The two post-war buildings make an allusion to the cloisters along the west side of the quadrangle but they hardly amount to a deferential architectural statement. They do, however, give order and cohesion to this internal space – the heart of the university. A sympathetic landscaping scheme has enhanced the area, which though generous in scale possesses a human and intimate sense of enclosure and serves as an admirable setting for such occasions as Graduation Days.

Sculptures and Trees

Sculpture has always been part of the exterior fabric at Queen's. The Lanyon Building was embellished with grotesque heads at the top of the tower, and carved angel busts lower down while the Old Library sports a series of zoomorphic water-spouts. Later came the shields, panels, corbels and label stops of the old Physics tower carved by Morris Harding as part of his commemorative series (much of it now gone) around the buildings of the quadrangle in 1948,[22] as well as his keystones and panel on the Whitla Hall.[23] Harding's contribution to the sculptural beauty of Queen's was acknowledged when he was awarded an honorary Master of Arts degree by the university in 1958.

In front of the Lanyon Building itself stands the university war memorial, designed by Sir Thomas Brock and executed by Arnold Wright in 1923. The group in bronze – a wounded youth being supported by a Winged Victory holding aloft a laurel crown – is symbolic of 'Sacrifice', and its granite pedestal records the names of Queen's men and women who gave their lives in two world wars. It was originally unveiled by the Duke of York on 21st July 1924 and re-dedicated on 8th November 1950.

The most recent sculptural addition at Queen's, dating from the 1980s, is the somewhat arcane installation on the lawn in front of the old library. The

Carved angel on Lanyon's entrance tower. Note the flying rib of the archway above it – a feature derived from Magdalen College, Oxford.

The War Memorial standing in front of the main university building. Designed by Sir Thomas Brock and executed by Arnold Wright in 1923.

granite slabs have an almost palaeolithic presence and were designed by Clifford Rainey and jointly sponsored by Queen's and the Arts Council of Northern Ireland. The work can be seen as a metaphor for the library – a quarry of learning. The unhewn granite is split open to reveal polished faces with inlaid cryptic symbols and lettering. The letters, a mirror image of the last line of a Michael Longley poem, read "Round this particular date I have drawn a circle".

Some years ago there arose the opportunity of providing a sculptural link between the university and the visit of Queen Victoria. The admirable suggestion, by Emeritus Professor Henri Godin, was to site a statue of the monarch on the blank gable on the south side of the quadrangle which bears her monogram in patterned brick. The full-sized statue was formerly situated high on the wall of Durham Street Primary School and it was offered to the university when the school was demolished. The offer was not taken up, however, and the statue is now at Rowallane House, Co Down, in the care of the National Trust.

The architectural and environmental quality of the main site also owes much to the trees that fringe the lawns along University Road and University Square. The chestnuts and limes are essential to the experience; other trees too, though departed, belong to the history of the university.

The Queen's Elms survive in name only, as the student halls on the Malone Road. Originally 'Queen's Elms' was a terrace of private houses, built by Thomas Jackson in 1859 on the site of the present Students' Union and designed to respond to the Tudor front of the college opposite. The terrace with its line of elms along University Road was acquired by the university early this century for use as a students' hostel. The eponymous trees did not long survive the arrival of the Students' Union, however, and they were replaced by the present silver birches. Their demise was apparently due to old age. They had doubtless been part of the "beauty of the natural setting" which had diversified the royal route to Queen's College and were probably old when Queen Victoria made her visit.

A fairy thorn provides a curious footnote in the annals of Queen's. When the Arts building in the south wing was completed in 1934 it was found that the thorn tree on the south side was overshadowing the bay window of the Senate Room and the contractor was instructed to remove it. Irish superstition has it that cutting down a fairy thorn brings bad luck and so the workmen refused. The tree was spared but its roots had been so disturbed by the excavations of the foundations that it died shortly afterwards. Nevertheless folklore persists concerning the incident; it has even been suggested that the alignment of the entire south wing was influenced by the position of the tree.

The Andrews Tree has similarly acquired an almost legendary status and it survived until the 1950s. Thomas Andrews was appointed Vice-President of

The original Queen's Elms terrace built in 1859 to the designs of Thomas Jackson, and demolished in 1963 to make way for the present Students' Union.

Queen's College at its foundation in 1845 and also Professor of Medicine and it was his habit to work in the shade of a large laburnum tree outside the Chemistry Department in the quadrangle. Although a slip was grown from the original tree it did not live to maturity and was removed in the 1980s. Recently the suggestion has been made that "perhaps it would be an appropriate and symbolic link with the past and an act of faith in the future to plant another Andrews Tree." [24]

Buildings in Elmwood

On 14th May 1926 the foundation stone of a fine new building for the recently created Faculty of Agriculture was laid in Elmwood Avenue by Lord Craigavon, the Prime Minister of Northern Ireland. The designs for the Agriculture Building as it was then (now the Geosciences Building) were by the architects to the Northern Ireland Ministry of Finance. Designed in a pleasing Georgian style with nice details such as the swags over circular windows, reminiscent of those on Wren's fountain court at Hampton Court Palace, and a rusticated brick doorway, the building was formally opened on

Above: an interior view of the former Agriculture Building (now the Geosciences Building) on Elmwood Avenue.

Right: the former Agriculture Building (now the Geosciences Building), built in the 1920s to the designs of the architects to the Northern Ireland Ministry of Finance. Photographed in 1949 before an additional storey was built in the 1950s.

A view of the east end of the Geology Building, Elmwood Avenue, designed by John MacGeagh and opened in 1954.

6th July 1928 by the Duke of Abercorn, Governor of Northern Ireland. Originally it was finished with a heavy cornice and parapet, but was given an additional storey in the 1950s, a development which had apparently been planned from the start. The interiors include an impressive double return stairway with Roman Doric columns and good contemporary iron balustrading. Each wing contains an octagonal lightwell, with a fair-faced rustic brick interior finish to the walls, an unusual treatment for the time. The original design, nominally the work of the ministry's chief architect Roland Ingleby Smith, working in conjunction with the university's consultant architect R.M. Close, was probably by T.F.O. Rippingham, the most gifted designer on Smith's staff. Certainly it was Rippingham who, as chief architect in his own right, was officially responsible some years later for the design of the additional storey in 1952, another instance of an architect extending his own work, reminiscent of the case of W.H. Lynn at the old library. The laboratory and lecture theatre to the rear was added in a modern style to designs prepared by Ostick and Williams in 1974 when converting the Agriculture Building to the Department of Geography.

The Geology Building designed in 1949 by John MacGeagh with Edward Maufe again as consultant was the next building venture on Elmwood Avenue. It was officially opened on 30th April 1954 by Sir Edward Bailey, a leading geologist of his time. The building was planned as the first unit of an intended group which was to face into a great central quadrangle opening southwards to Elmwood Avenue.[25] It was designed in a style that respected the neo-Georgian Agriculture Building but was also contemporary in inspiration. As J.K. Charlesworth, the first Professor of Geology at Queen's, remarked however, "Its fresh Georgian treatment, well adapted to a school of science, is flexible enough to adjoin any future neighbours, however designed".[26] His words had a prophetic ring indeed as the grand Beaux Arts scheme for the area was eventually abandoned and the building's future neighbour, the new Students' Union of 1966, was to be built in an almost uncompromisingly modern idiom. The Geology Building itself has remained unfinished in detail: urns were intended to be set on the corner pedestals and a sculpted figure to stand in the central niche of the end elevation where unworked blocks of stone are now to be seen.

The David Keir Building

The post Second World War era saw the university embark on two very large projects side by side on Stranmillis Road. The first of them was the David Keir Building, built to house Engineering, Chemistry and the Biological Sciences. The new building, named after the Vice-Chancellor who had acquired the site for it, is monumental in scale ("elephantine" some would have it[27]), essentially modern and utilitarian in purpose, yet styled in neo-

The original design for the David Keir building on Stranmillis Road, drawn for the architects Lanchester and Lodge by the noted perspective artist Cyril Farey.

Georgian rustic brick and Portland stone. Axially planned, it spreads between the two diverging roads, Malone and Stranmillis, with long corridors and somewhat sterile courtyards between them, and a curved north entrance block at the prow, mostly lost from public view and rarely used since the expected clearance of the nineteenth-century houses at that angle of the site did not happen. Though somewhat conservative in style by the 1950s, the long sweeping, rather *moderne* horizontal lines of the Stranmillis Road frontage are nicely offset by the towered entrance where the vertical elements seem to recall not only other recent university monuments in England, as in the case of the pyramidal roofed tower, but also seem to suggest, to local eyes at any rate, an allusion to mediaeval Irish architecture in the twin curved bays flanking the arched gateway.

The David Keir Building was designed by Dr Thomas Lodge of the London firm Lanchester and Lodge who were appointed in 1950, the year their monumental Beaux Arts scheme for Leeds University was completed. Construction started in 1952 and five years later the part of the building for Engineering was occupied, quickly followed by Chemistry in 1958. The whole building was already in use some time before its official opening by the Duke of Edinburgh on 21st May 1959: "A Vision Realised", ran the headlines at the time.[28] During his tour of the new building the Duke tried his hand at organic chemistry and successfully carried out an experiment which produced a new coloured compound – chloro-morpholinovinyl-napthoquinone – the first time the experiment had been carried out with the particular compounds used by the Duke. After adding two clear solutions to a yellow liquid His Royal Highness grinned broadly when "the desired result", a purple solution, became evident, and commented "It would appear the experiment has been a complete success".[29]

The Ashby Building

No sooner had one vast complex on Stranmillis Road been completed than work started on a complementary and equally massive project next door. The Ashby Institute (now Ashby Building) was initially the responsibility of the Joint Authority for Higher Technological Studies, a joint body formed by the University and Belfast Corporation. It was built to house the Departments of Electrical Engineering, Mechanical Engineering and Engineering Mathematics. Work started on site in early 1960 and five years later, on 7th May 1965, the completed building was opened by Sir Eric Ashby. This "educational palace in brilliant white concrete and glass", as the press hailed it,[30] marked something of an architectural watershed for Belfast in general and Queen's in particular. The contrast between what was 'old' and what was 'new' in post-war architecture was probably nowhere more apparent than in the university's two buildings standing side by side on Stranmillis Road. The Ashby uncompromisingly reflected the nature of a forward looking establishment while the Keir by comparison seemed to suggest a sterile academicism which its function hardly warranted.

The Ashby was the work of the Manchester architects Cruickshank & Seward, the partner in charge being W.A. Gibbon. The design revealed a precisely detailed and well organised exposition of functional requirements, appropriate to an institute of advanced engineering. It consists of three distinct architectural masses – an eleven-storey tower containing classrooms and offices, a two-storey block containing heavy mechanical engineering laboratories, and a smaller lecture theatre block at the foot of the tower – all designed as separate structures but linked at ground and first floor levels by the glazed circulation spine. All are constructed of reinforced concrete made from limestone quarried at Glenarm in Co. Antrim which produced an unusually white finish. Balancing the cool colour of the concrete, the window frames and other woodwork were made of varnished mahogany. The horizontal pivot windows, manufactured by a local firm included, incidentally, the largest windows of their type ever produced in the United Kingdom, some of them as high as 12 feet.

The idiom is now termed 'International Modern', that universally common style of architecture at the time that exhibited largely clean lines and flat façades, but there was a faint attempt to jazz things up by the introduction of a storey-height raised diamond pattern applied to part of the tower block. The two-storeyed laboratories have a sculptural roofscape with cyclindrical and cubic forms reminiscent of the work of the influential French architect Le Corbusier. Further relief was added by the Mourne granite panels which face the ground floor walls of the tower. The whole complex may have been somewhat out of scale with its surroundings but it was an assured, indeed dramatic building, which still forms one of the most significant landmarks in

The faceted diamond patterning on the Ashby Building.

The Ashby Building viewed from Stranmillis Road, photographed at the time of completion in 1965.

Belfast. It is regrettable however that some of the grass around the building, which was in itself an element in the design, providing the only bright colour to be seen, has been removed from the site in recent years to provide car-parking space.

Expansion in the 60s

The Ashby Institute was just part of the university's ambitious development programme of the 1960s. Another element of that programme was the Students' Union building which was designed by local architects Ostick and Williams in 1962 and opened in 1967. It is a straightforward if undistinguished example of modern architecture of the period, although the attempt to design the end of the return wing on Elmwood Avenue in a manner complementary to the earlier Geology Building may be noted, as may two examples of applied art within it. The ground floor of the Elmwood Avenue entrance hall contains a mural by the design associates Desmond Kinney and Ralph Dobson of Belfast. Coloured concrete with inlaid mosaic of ceramics, glass and beach stones, forms an abstract landscape which includes mountains, rocks, plants and a symbol of the sun. A second mural, on the wall of the debating hall foyer, is an entirely abstract composition of shaped white planks on a pastel background, and was the result of a nation-wide competition for students in schools and colleges, won by Rod Suttcliffe from Hammersmith College of Art and Building.

Architecturally, however, the Union is a building which perhaps does not quite rise to the occasion, facing the main Lanyon Building, and it still elicits feelings of regret for the passing of the old Dutch-gabled Queen's Elms Halls of Residence, originally designed as a terrace of houses by Thomas Jackson in 1859, which was demolished in 1963 to make way for the Union.

The same could now be said of the huge Medical Biology Centre of 1963–68 facing the other end of Elmwood Avenue on Lisburn Road. Designed by the firm of Samuel Stevenson & Sons for the Departments of Anatomy, Bio-Chemistry and Physiology formerly housed on the main University site, and opened in 1968, it impressed enough to receive a Civic Trust award in 1969. "The building group masses well in its setting, with the transition between the three two-storey wings and the ten-storey slab being particularly successful" and "choice of materials is nicely restrained" went the assessor's comments at the time[31] but it is hard to look on it now without sensing the loss of its predecessor on the site, the old Institute for the Deaf and Dumb and Blind of 1843–5, by Charles Lanyon, which was demolished in 1963.

The new Queen's Elms Halls of Residence built at Holyrood, Malone Road, was also part of the 1960s development programme. Started in 1961 to the designs of Cruickshank & Seward of Manchester, architects of the Ashby Building, the partner in charge here being J.R.G. Seward, the complex was one of the University's most successful post-war projects. Brick-clad eleven-storey residential tower blocks are informally disposed over an undulating site, each at a different angle, with a lower irregularly shaped dining hall block as a central focus of the group.

The skilful landscaping designed by Brenda Colvin includes a small serpentine artificial lake and employs well-rounded forms to mellow and set off the angular geometry of the buildings. While not intended to be a major architectural *tour de force* the complex did set out to provide an appropriate setting for the student way of life in buildings which respected the natural beauty of the site and in that it was a complete success. It should remain so as long as the later small scale additions are not increased in

A view of Queen's Elms Halls of Residence at 78 Malone Road, showing the dining hall block and one of the residential towers, designed by Cruickshank and Seward and opened in 1967.

number. The original complex of four halls was officially opened on 13th March 1967 by the then Prime Minister of Northern Ireland, Captain Terence O'Neill, and later that year work started on a fifth residential block, the three-storeyed Sinton Hall designed by the same architects and completed in 1970.

The last new building completed by Queen's in the 1960s was the Science Library on a site between Chlorine Gardens and Lennoxvale. Designed in 1965 by Twist and Whitley of Cambridge and completed in 1969, it was built using the S.E.A.C. system of building, originally developed in England by the South Eastern Architects' Collaboration under the sponsorship of Hertfordshire County Council. It was the university's first venture into in-dustrialised architecture and their success with it in this instance gained an R.I.B.A. award in 1970.

Queen's at The Royal Victoria Hospital

A few miles to the west of the main campus the six-storey high Micro-biology Building was erected by Queen's in the grounds of the Royal Victoria Hospital on Grosvenor Road, to designs prepared in 1961 by the distinguished architects Sir Hugh Casson and Neville Condor of London. It came into use in May 1965 but was not formally opened until 6th April

The Microbiology Building at the Royal Victoria site.

The Science Library viewed from Lennoxvale, designed in 1965 by Twist and Whitley and completed in 1969.

Sir Hugh Casson's perspective sketch for the Microbiology Building of 1961–5 designed in partnership with Neville Condor.

1967 when the ceremony was performed by Lord Erskine, the Governor of Northern Ireland. It stands impressively on its site, and the treatment of its concrete textures and finishes and the layout of its terraces and abutments is masterly. It is one of the finer new buildings commissioned by the university.

Queen's had established itself on the Royal Victoria site some years earlier when it built the Institute of Pathology there to designs prepared in 1930 by Captain James Young of the firm of Young and MacKenzie; it was opened on 7th July 1933 by Lord Craigavon, the Prime Minister of Northern Ireland. An additional storey which had been anticipated from the start was added by the same architects in 1949.

The Institute of Pathology was followed by the Institute of Clinical Science alongside it, designed by the London architects Easton and Robertson in 1949. It was built in two parts, divided by the main hospital road and linked at first floor level by a bridge of unusual design. It was comprised of deep girders constructed of butterfly units of tubular steel welded together, with one end of the bridge hinged and the other mounted on rollers to allow for movement. The ornamental caduceus, based on the emblem of the Babylonian god Ningizzida, which decorates the centre of the bridge was modelled in anodised aluminium by S. Niczewski, and the emblems which decorate the main doorway to the east block were by the English sculptress Miss Mary Spencer-Watson. The building was opened on 7th May 1954 by Lord Wakehurst, Governor of Northern Ireland.

The front entrance to the Institute of Pathology, designed by Young and MacKenzie, 1930–3.

Historic Buildings Acquired by Queen's

Apart from the new buildings which the university has commissioned over the years, Queen's has also acquired other properties from time to time and adapted them for university use. A number of these are of architectural interest or have special historical associations. Among the more important of these in the vicinity of the campus are the following.

University Square

This three-storey range of red brick houses is perhaps the best formal terrace in Ulster. The main run of twenty-seven houses, now numbered 4–30, was built in portions between 1848 and 1853 while the taller set of three at the west end, numbered 1–3, came much later, in 1870.

The ground, part of the lands known as 'The Plains', was laid out for private residential development for the owner Jane Gregg as part of an overall

A detail of the bridge at the Institute of Clinical Science showing the decorative emblem by the artist Niczewski.

plan by Charles Lanyon, as revealed in deeds for the various properties and as publicised in a newspaper advertisement at the time:

Notice to builders. The Land adjoining Queen's College, having been judiciously laid out for building by Mr Lanyon, is to be Let on lease. Early application is recommended, as several Professors having already secured ground for Houses, the most desirable sites will be disposed of, without reserve. Liberal encouragement will be given to Builders wishing to engage several sites.[32]

The street was, incidentally, originally intended to be called Victoria Square, as the earliest deeds indicate, but in the end it was named University Square, even though Belfast was not building a university then but a college. The epithet 'college' had, however, already been used in street names elsewhere in Belfast. Among the earliest private owners of properties in the terrace were Rev. John Edgar and Rev. Dr Killen, professors in the Presbyterian Assembly's College; and Cranston Gregg, the contractor for the Queen's College.

A view of University Square showing some of the terrace houses built between 1848 and 1853, with a glimpse of Charles Lanyon's Presbyterian College (1852–3) at the end of the street.

Although Lanyon was responsible for the layout of the street and the block, the detailed design of the houses was probably not his work. As early as 1847 indentures had stipulated that the elevational treatment of the houses had to follow that of Glenfield Place, a terrace then being built at what is now 121–135 Ormeau Road, but whose architect is not known. That model was however stuccoed which raises the possibility that the same treatment was intended for University Square, as indeed some projecting mouldings and the unresolved junctions between some doorways and corner quoins might suggest, but in the end the brickwork was left uncovered.

Three-storeyed, with painted dressings and recessed Doric porches, the main terrace of original houses stands as a fairly regular and unified composition despite some initial variations in house widths, door positions, and alignment of frontages, as well as some later bay window additions and other minor alterations. Some of the later doors and fanlights with decorative leaded glass of the early 1900s are, incidentally, very attractive in their own right and are well worth retaining since they add a delightful variety to the façades.

When numbers 1 to 3 were built in 1870 it was to a somewhat different design from the earlier houses, being taller and chunkier in a more characteristically Victorian way rather than Georgian. They were designed by the Belfast firm of Thomas Jackson and Son, and indeed Jackson himself may well have been the architect responsible for the design of the original terrace.

A typical front doorway in University Square, built between 1848 and 1853, which also shows some of the later modifications to fanlights and doors.

Elmwood Hall

The Elmwood Hall was originally Elmwood Presbyterian Church, designed in 1859 by a talented amateur architect John Corry, a member of a well known family of building contractors and shipowners. It was opened in 1862.

Corry displayed here an unusually exotic artistic ability inspired no doubt by the writings of John Ruskin. Lombardo-Venetian in style, with a lofty tower and spire which was not actually erected until 1872, this is a very rich example of High Victorian architecture, with arcading, coupled windows, carved friezes and decorative corbel courses. The capitals of the loggia present a fine series of plant studies each one different, possibly the work of the Fitzpatricks who were the most accomplished stone-carvers in Belfast at the time. The carvings are very much in Ruskinian taste, as are the 'eyes of coloured marble' as he would have termed the coloured stone discs which appear above them.

There is a wide and spacious interior with good plasterwork but the fine pulpit and other furnishings were removed when the building ceased to be used as a church in the 1970s,[33] as were the stained glass windows, now replaced by pseudo-Georgian glazing. The additions to the rear were built in

An 'eye of coloured marble' above one of the carved capitals at the Elmwood Hall.

An elevational drawing of Elmwood Presbyterian Church (now the Elmwood Hall) prepared for the completion of the tower in 1872, by John Corry the original architect. The attached letter relates to the presentation of the drawing to the congregation of the church by a descendant of the architect in 1951. It includes a sentence which reads "There may be differences of opinion on the subject of his skill as an architect but there can be no question about John Corry's extraordinary competence as a draughtsman."

1866 and originally comprised school rooms and a lecture hall, while the building attached to the south side was built as the manse in 1872. The boundary railings, gates and piers to the front were all added in 1873 to the designs of the original architect John Corry.

Queen's acquired the property around 1972 and with great success converted it into a concert hall, an admirable project which was carried out with great care and sympathy for the old building and thereby set the standard for the university's subsequent treatment of the historic buildings in its care. The tower and spire were painstakingly restored in 1984.

Lennoxvale House

Lennoxvale House was built in 1876 for John Ward of the world famous printing and publishing firm Marcus Ward and Company. A substantial three-storey house of Scrabo sandstone laid out on an informal plan, it has a large gothic arched porch as the central feature on its south front. It was designed by the Belfast firm of architects Young and MacKenzie, and was probably the

Lennoxvale House, Lennoxvale, built in 1876 to the designs of Young and MacKenzie; photographed around 1906.

One of the ornamental lakes in the grounds of Lennoxvale House. Photographed by Country Life *in 1949.*

work of the founder of the firm Robert Young who also built a sandstone house of Gothic character for himself in Chichester Park in the 1870s. The style was uncommon for purely domestic work in Ulster, most houses of this size at the time being in a form of Italianate style (as can be seen in some of the other villas in Lennoxvale, designed by the same firm). Robert Young, incidentally, was one of Charles Lanyon's earliest pupils and after completing his apprenticeship became his principal assistant for a few years until he left around 1849. He dealt mainly with railway work at that time but it is possible that he could have been involved with the Queen's College commission at some stage given the scale and duration of that job.

The garden house at Lennoxvale House, designed by Young and MacKenzie, c 1890.

Here at Lennoxvale House there are good naturalistic stone carvings of foliage and animals, such as the squirrel and the bird to each side of one window. Nearby in the grounds is a very attractive garden house built in the angle of the orchard walls. It has a lower storey of red brick, octagonal in plan, with an over-sailing black and white timbered upper floor. Elsewhere in the garden is what appears to be a well-head in much weathered white marble, now used as a flower tub. It is carved with magnificent sprays of acanthus foliage at the corners and bears the Hapsburg crest of a double-headed eagle with crowns. It was probably brought here from the continent by a later owner of the house, Sir William Whitla who was a great traveller and "an inveterate collector of bric a brac and *objets d'art*" as one biographer has put it.[34] In this instance his collecting instinct has provided Ulster with a very rare architectural treasure.

Marble well-head in the garden of Lennoxvale House, probably brought from the continent by Sir William Whitla.

Queen's acquired the house and property when it was bequeathed to it by Sir William in 1934 to be the residence of future vice-chancellors of the university. Aside from its architectural interest Lennoxvale House is also of note for its beautiful gardens, covering some seven acres, which follow the curves of a deep valley in which two lakes are hidden. As *Country Life* remarked at the time of the centenary of Queen's opening, "The presence of such a landscape garden in a suburb of the city is as surprising as it is delightful. No other vice-chancellor, and indeed, no head of an Oxford or Cambridge College, can boast such a lovely garden attached to his office."[35]

Notes

1. *Northern Whig*, 22 December 1849.
2. The Royal visit was extensively reported in *Belfast News-Letter*, 14 August 1849.
3. As recorded in *Belfast News-Letter*, 27 July and 7 August 1849 ('Preparations for Her Majesty's Visit to Belfast').
4. T.W. Moody and J.C. Beckett, *Queen's, Belfast 1845–1949. The history of a university*, London, 1959, p 84.
5. *Ibid*, p 99.
6. Denis Ireland, *From the Jungle of Belfast. Footnotes to history 1904–72*, Belfast, 1973, p 40.
7. Moody and Beckett, *op cit*, p 112.
8. *Ibid*, p 111.
9. Such as the *Ecclesiologist* of April 1849, who thought that both the Belfast and the Galway colleges were "positively bad", though it may have been the absence of a chapel as much as anything that had prejudiced this view.
10. M. Craig, *The Architecture of Ireland from the earliest times to 1880*, London, 1982, p 298.
11. Philip Larkin, 'The Library I came to', *Gown Literary Supplement '84*, Belfast, 1984, p 3.
12. Moody and Beckett, *op cit*, p 438.
13. 'Notes on the brothers Lynn', in *Belfast Museum, Quarterly Notes*, No. XXXII, Spring 1916.
14. *The Builder*, 22 October 1910 (report on the competition).
15. *Ibid*.
16. Senate approval of MacGeagh's plans was recorded in *Belfast News-Letter*, 27 November 1936.
17. Moody and Beckett, *op cit*, p 536.
18. As quoted in *Belfast News-Letter*, 19 February 1949.
19. *Ibid*.
20. As quoted in *Belfast News-Letter*, 21 February 1949.
21. *Civic Trust Awards Report*, London, 1966, p 113.
22. The carvings at the old Physics tower represent the following, as identified in Morris Harding's own notes. South side of archway – main arms: The Queen's University in Ireland; quatrefoils, left to right: Sapientia and Justicia; spandrels, left to right: Arms of Sir Isaac Newton, and Arms of the Earl of Cork and Orrery. North side of archway – main arms: The Royal University in Ireland; panel of Tudor roses; spandrels, left to right: Arms of Lord Kelvin, and Arms of The Earl of Rosse; label stops, left to right: agriculture (potato foliage), and linen (flax foliage). Corbels within the archway – east side: England (Tudor roses), and Wales (leeks); west side: Ireland (shamrock), and Scotland (thistle); corners: only Canada (maple leaves) was completed, in north-west corner, leaving the rest of the series unfinished, but intended to be South Africa, New Zealand, and Australia.
23. The keystones of the Whitla Hall represent the following, as identified in Morris Harding's own notes – entrance front, left to right: Sir William Whitla's Arms, and the Arms of the Medical Profession; east side, left to right: rope, flax, tobacco, dairy farming, agriculture, aeroplane construction, shipbuilding; west side, left to right: law, science, biology, an owl, theology, engineering, literature.
24. Ivan Strahan, sub-editor, in *Queen's Letter*, Summer, 1994, Vol. 10 No. 2, p 11.
25. As explained in *Northern Whig*, 30 April 1954.
26. *Belfast News-Letter*, 29 September 1949, p 8.
27. Robert McKinstry for example, in 'Contemporary Architecture', *Causeway: The Arts in Ulster*, Belfast, 1971, p 29.
28. See *Belfast News-Letter*, 22 May 1959, p 11.
29. *Ibid*, p 10.
30. See *Belfast News-Letter*, 7 May 1965.
31. *Civic Trust Awards Report*, London, 1969, p 90.
32. *Northern Whig*, 17 March 1849.
33. Photographs of the interior can be seen in J. Dewar, *A History of Elmwood Church*, Belfast, 1900.
34. Cecil W. Kidd in 'Sir William Whitla: Profile of a Benefactor' *The Ulster Medical Journal*, December 1962.
35. *Country Life*, 9 September 1949, p 748.

Recent Additions to the Campus

New buildings erected by Queen's have included the following: the Physical Education Centre designed by Ostick and Williams in 1966 and completed in 1972 on a site within the Botanic Gardens; new buildings to house Applied Maths and Physics and the Computer Centre in a complex designed by Twist and Whitley in 1969 using the S.E.A.C. Mark 2a system and built in 1971–2 in the College Park area behind the main site; the Staff Common Room of 1970–2 by Cruickshank and Seward in College Gardens; the former Zoology and Botany building on Malone Road by H.A. Patton and Partners, 1973–6; the Whitla Medical Building of 1976 and the Department of Pharmacy Building of 1980, both adjacent to the Medical Biology Centre, Lisburn Road; a new building for the Department of Architecture by Ferguson and McIlveen in Chlorine Gardens, 1985; the Palaeoecology Building in Fitzwilliam Street by Samuel Stevenson and Sons, 1986; and several new student residences, namely the new Riddel Hall at the Queen's Elms site designed by Houston and Beaumont in 1977, Sir Arthur Vick House in Sans Souci Park, designed by Colin Deane Partnership, and opened in 1987, Grant House, Malone Road, by Macrae Hanlon Spence, Guthrie House, Fitzwilliam Street by Knox and Markwell, and Shaftesbury Hall at the Queen's Elms site, by Ferguson and McIlveen, all opened in 1991, and the Sir Rowland Wright Hall in Sans Souci Park, by Robinson and Patterson, opened in 1992; and the Northern Ireland Technology Centre at Cloreen Park, designed by Samuel Stevenson and Sons and opened on 29th May 1990 by the Duke of Kent. It was built to house under one roof a range of design and experimental departments previously housed in the David Keir Building and the Ashby Building.

Listed Buildings

Buildings owned by Queen's, in the vicinity of the campus, which were statutorily listed by 1995, are as follows: The Lanyon Building, Old Library, Music Department, Old Physics Building, the War Memorial, and the Sir William Whitla Hall, all on the main site; The Geosciences Building, and the Geology Building, both on Elmwood Avenue; 1–30 University Square; The Elmwood Hall, University Road; Lennoxvale House, Lennoxvale; 1, 7–9, 11 and 12, 15, 17 and 18, 21 and 22, 25, 32 College Gardens; 6, 8, 12, 14, 18–26 College Green; 2–8 Fitzwilliam Street; 8 Malone Road; 5–19, 26–50 Mount Charles; 42–48, 71–75 University Road; The Mulhouse Building, Royal Victoria Hospital; 26 Sans Souci Park; 185 and 185A Stranmillis Road; 7 University Terrace; 14–16 Upper Crescent.

Acknowledgements

The authors gratefully acknowledge assistance from the following: Michael Smallman and the staff of the special collections in The Library at Queen's; Karen Latimer, Architecture Librarian; Hubert Martin and the staff of the Estates and Buildings Office; Ivan Ewart and the staff of the Audio Visual Services at Queen's; and Ivan Strahan of the Information Office, Gerry Power of the Alumni Office, and Mervyn Farrell of the 'Queen's 150 Office'. Thanks are also due to Karen Agnew and Roslyn Clarke who typed the manuscript.

Sources of Information

Sources of information included the following: original architectural drawings, in the collection of the university in the case of the original Lanyon Building, and primarily in the Building Control Office in Belfast City Hall in the case of most subsequent developments; deeds to university properties; press reports on the laying of foundation stones and on the official opening of buildings, to be found in the *Belfast News-Letter*, *Northern Whig*, and *Belfast Telegraph*; reports on the progress of building work, and general articles, to be found in the architectural press, primarily in *The Builder* and *The Irish Builder and Engineer*. The following books and articles were also particularly useful: "The Queen's University, Belfast. A Centenary Celebration", in *Country Life*, 9 September 1949, pp 744–748; T.W. Moody and J.C. Beckett, *Queen's, Belfast 1845–1949. The history of a university*, London, 1959; Hugh Dixon and David Evans, *Historic buildings . . . in the vicinity of the Queen's University of Belfast*, U.A.H.S., Belfast, 1975; Paul Larmour, *Belfast, An Illustrated Architectural Guide*, Friar's Bush Press, Belfast, 1987; and B. Walker and A. McCreary, *Degrees of Excellence. The Story of Queen's, Belfast 1845–1995*, Belfast, 1994.

Sources of Illustrations

The illustrations listed here are identified by their page number and their position on the page, the positions being noted in alphabetical order left to right and top to bottom on the page: frontispiece, 13a & b, 14a, 15a & b, 18, 19a & b, 22, 25, 26, 27, 29a, 31, 33, 34a, b & c, 35, 36, 37a & b, 39, 40, 42a, 43, 46a, 49, 50a, 51a & b, 52, 53a & b, 57a & b, and back cover, all by Paul Larmour; 11a & b, 14b, 20b, 23, 24a, 28, and front cover, all by David Evans; 7, 8a & b, 9, 10, 16, 29b, 30, 32, 41, 42b, 47, 55, 56, all courtesy of Queen's Library; 12a & 17b, courtesy of Ivan Strahan; 17a, courtesy NIHE; 20a, from *The Book of the Fete*, Queen's College, Belfast, 1907; 21, from *The Graphic*, 22 August 1874; 38, courtesy of Donald Shanks; 45, from the collection of the university, 50b by J.R. Watson; 5, 50c, courtesy of the Estates and Buildings Office at Queen's; 54, courtesy of Ian Gailey.